Thrive

Autumn Outdoor Nature Activities
For Children and Families

The Early Years
2 - 8 years

Gillian Powell M.Ed.

978-1-912328-94-9

Copyright 2021© Gillian Powell

All intellectual property rights including copyright, design right and publishing rights rest with the author Gillian Powell. No part of this book may be copied, reproduced, stored or transmitted in any way including any written, electronic, recording, or photocopying without written permission of the author. Illustrations and images by the author. Other images used are freely available in the public domain or purchased from stock photography. Published in Ireland by Orla Kelly Publishing.

Acknowledgements

Thank you to my husband Tom.

Thank you also to Steve, Dave, Mary, Suzanne, Antony, Philip, Lisa, Conor and Leah.

To Darragh, Dylan and Sophie, and all the little people who made this project special and to all the children and families who have inspired me over the years.

To my wonderful colleagues in early years education, may they be blessed and of course to my wider family and friends.

A special thanks to Liz Casey who gave guidance at all times and of course to Orla Kelly Publishing who made this a lovely experience.

I live in a beautiful part of Ireland and walk in the public woods and forests of Bandon and Innishannon. I would like to thank special friends Claire and Stanley Deane and also Roy and Jenny Kingston for their generosity in sharing their beautiful farmland and forests.

In memory of my mother and father and an outdoor childhood in West Waterford with my brother Ben and sister Betty.

Contents

Acknowledgements	iii
Introduction	1
Creative Activities	12
Maths Activities	26
Developing Language	36
Well Being Activities	46
Halloween Fun	48
Emotional Activities	63
References	66

"Autumn carries more gold in its pocket than all the other seasons."
Jim Bishop

Introduction

Autumn is considered the second Spring in some countries. It is a time of glorious colour when nature prepares us for the darkness of winter with a show of splendour.

For me, it is all about the trees and the glory of trees of all shapes and sizes, and the wonder of leaves. Leaves are a source of eternal fascination for children and can provide opportunities for exploring and thinking about everything.

Thrive seeks to help parents and early-year teachers enjoy time outdoors, in all weathers, in the garden, in a field, in a forest or at the ocean.

In my thirty-two years as an early years educator and researcher in West Cork in Ireland, I have observed that children are never happier than when they are out of doors. This is especially true in Autumn.

In October and early November, the best of any day in an early years setting was getting outside amongst the gold and red leaves. There was no substitute for the feeling of being alive when you jumped in a pile of leaves or splashed through the puddles. This book explores activities that encourage and enhance children's holistic development. More than that, these activities provide opportunities for you to connect with your children and the world around you wherever you live.

In some cultures, Autumn is a time of thanksgiving for the bounty of the earth; it does sustain us, perhaps this is a time for all of us to be grateful for "all things, bright and beautiful". We live in an abundant universe; Autumns gifts are ample proof of that.

Play is the most important thing in any child's life, so free play is vital in any outdoor adventure, but this series of books is about turning play opportunities into opportunities to learn. This is best done gently and encouragingly.

Thrive activities will help you and yours to a sense of emotional, mental and physical health and well-being in the modern world. Research in "Science Advance", where researchers built a forest floor daycare, shows that play outside amongst the biodiverse microbes, after just one month, changed the children's immune system. Thrive activities will also provide wonderful opportunities for cognitive development. Pull on the boots, wrap up and let's explore outside in Autumn.

What you need

- ☑ Comfortable clothes and a change of clothes.
- ☑ Waterproof coat – fleece-lined in cold weather.
- ☑ Waterproof pull-ups (fleece-lined), if it is cold.
- ☑ Wellies.
- ☑ Healthy snacks are necessary for any trip with children.
- ☑ Fruit and a sandwich.
- ☑ Drink – Water.
- ☑ A flask of tea and a snack for the adults is always a welcome treat.
- ☑ Treasure Bag – A special bag to collect the treasures of the walk.
- ☑ Knapsack.
- ☑ Clothing for colder, wetter weather.

Look for:
- Clothes that protect your children from rain, wind and cold.
- Clothes that are easy to put on and off.
- Allow room for climbing, running and jumping.
- Clothes that stand up to wear and tear.
- Create layers that can be taken off if temperature or conditions change.
- Always bring a change of clothes.

Remember the following

Be safe.
Run free and have adventures but make sure you take care.
Leave no trace.
Be considerate of places and other people.

Autumn Tree

I think that I shall never see
A poem lovely as a tree
- Joyce Kilmer.

Prompt Questions For Children

Things take time is my mantra in the forest, and I learned this lately from a great outdoor educator in Donegal, Sally Parks. These questions should be collaborative and gentle like the tree itself.

Sight
What do you see?
How many colours can we find?

Sound
What can you hear?
Choose words to describe what the wind sounds like?
Is it rustling through the trees?
Is it whispering?

Touch
Can you feel the trunk?
This could involve a group hug of your favourite tree.
Can you feel the bark?

Smell
Can you smell the tree?

What does it smell like?

Take all the time in the world. The tree is not going anywhere.

5 Common Leaves of Autumn - Europe (Labels attached to each leaf).

Clockwise – (1) Sycamore, (2) Ash, (3) Oak, (4) Beach and (5) Horse Chestnut.

Outdoor Activities

Gratitude-

A thanksgiving treasure hunt

Find something you like

Find something that is your favourite colour

Discover something new

Find something that other people will enjoy

Find something that feels soft

Find something that makes you feel safe

Find something beautiful

Find a place that you love

Find someone you are grateful for

Find something you can use

Find something that makes you feel safe

Explore The Unknown!

Creative Activities

Leaf painting, leaf collages, leaf rubbing, Autumn suncatchers, leaf people, leaf animals.

Autumn is simply the best time to do creative activities with children. The leaves are glorious, and some simple paints and crayons create gorgeous decorations for your home.

Leaf Painting

Materials – What you need

Paints, brushes, paper of varying sizes and a variety of leaves.

Directions

Collect a variety of leaves outdoors. You can set up a painting area outside if you wish.

Paint the leaves and encourage the children to be as creative and messy as they like. Discuss the colours and then give your children space to develop their own creativity.

You can simply stick painted leaves on a page and add some fingerprints, or you can press the leaves on a page and lift them off to reveal a wonderful leaf print.

An Autumn leaf collage, this is a great collaborative family activity.

Leaf Rubbing

A leaf rubbing takes a lot of strength and is helpful for developing hand muscles.

Materials – What you need

A collection of leaves and some fat crayons and white paper.

Directions

Collect a variety of leaves.

Place a piece of white paper over the leaves.

Place the crayons on their side.

Rub vigorously over the leaves, and a pattern emerges.

Autumn Suncatchers

Materials – What you need

A collection of leaves, with a variety of shapes and colours.

Transparent contact paper or sticky back plastic. (Used for covering school books).

Sellotape.

Directions

Collect a wide variety of leaves and stick them on to transparent contact paper.

Use sellotape to stick on to your glass door or window.

Autumn Suncatcher

Leaf people, birds and animals

Leaf Birds

Materials – What you need
Leaves, seeds, a marker and googly eyes.

Directions
Talk about the animal or bird your child would create and look at photos of that bird or animal. Talk about the facial features, such as eyes, nose and ears. Talk about the hands and legs and how your creatures will move.

Create your leaf creatures, allow your child to dictate the creation.

A leaf stag, with impressive antlers.

Extended Learning

Leaves are an ideal tool for extending learning. This rainbow collage involves collecting and classifying very many leaves according to their size and colour.

Learning can further be extended to include matching the leaf to the name of its parent tree.

Autumn Dress Up - Butterfly Wings

Materials – What you need

Scissors, glue, cardboard, string and a large collection of leaves.

Directions

Cut out a butterfly shape suitably sized to your child.

Put a generous amount of glue on the cardboard wings and stick on the leaves.

Attach two long pieces of string to go round the child's shoulders.

Autumn Crown

Materials – What you need
Scissors, a strip of card to go round your child's head, masking tape, glue, a decorative ribbon and autumn leaves.

Directions

Put a generous amount of glue on the strip of card. Arrange the leaves on the card.

Staple or glue the strip of ribbon on to the card to secure the leaves.

Measure your child's head and use masking tape to create the crown.

Child's Autumn Crown

Autumn Leaf Decorations

Materials – What you need
Leaves, clothes pegs and string.

Autumn leaves string creations

Add a large needle and a piece of wood, and you have an impressive decoration. Adult assistance required.

Extended Learning – Emergent Literacy

To extend the learning, you can print letters on the leaves and leave love and joy messages.

Children's names and their own mark-making and creations could be displayed in your home.

Maths Activities

Juliet Robinson, in her wonderful book Messy Maths (2017), talks about it being a mathematical world. She points out that for young children, maths is not just a cognitive process. "It is also a social, emotional and physical experience". It is up to us adults to be playful and lead the way. A problem shared is a problem halved, the outdoor world is full of problems, patterns, symmetries and textures. If we collaborate with children, listen to their questions, and provide playful and spontaneous mathematical conversations, we may encourage an early love of maths that will last a lifetime.

Autumn provides lots of counting opportunities.

Collect acorns and swap the nuts for colourful marbles.

Marble acorns – This is an excellent activity for developing fine motor skills.

Autumn Leaf Chart

Autumn Leaf Chart

Materials – What you need

A collection of different colour leaves.

A large piece of white card, glue, a black marker, a ruler, crayons.

Directions

Collect a variety of leaves.

Collaborate with your child to draw the chart – colours on the horizontal line and numbers on the vertical line.

Count, classify and glue as you go.

Enjoy using the ruler.

Display and encourage discussion of the colours, and numbers of leaves. (Talk about the 40 shades of green).

Extended Learning

Create a chart with big leaves and small leaves.

Seed Numbers

Materials – What you need

Seeds, these are Ash seeds, collect whatever is in your area.

Glue and white card.

Directions

Collect seeds.

Write numbers on the white card.

Glue the seeds on to the outline of each number and display for playful conversations.

Match acorns to the number displayed.

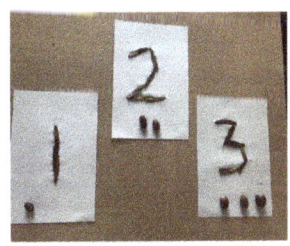

Leaf Shapes

Materials – What you need

Leaves, sticks, glue.

Directions

Arrange sticks into a triangle shape. Glue on leaves.

Photograph and display.

Triangle

Leaf Square

Materials – What you need

White paper, glue and lollipop sticks.

Directions

Create a square shape with the lollipop sticks and attach leaves.

Counting in Pairs

Notice that children have a pair of shoes and this is an ideal opportunity to count in pairs.

2+2+2+2+2

The animals went in two by two

The animals went in two by two,

The animals went in two by two, hurrah, hurrah.

The animals went in two by two, hurrah, hurrah.

The animals went in two by two,
The squirrel and the rabbit too
And they all went into the ark, for to get out of the rain.

Extended Learning

The animals went in three by three, four by four etc...Think of animals that rhyme with the relevant number.

The animals went in three by three; the animals went in three by three; the animals went in three by three, the gorilla and the chimpanzee, etc.

The animals went in four by four, the hippopotamus stuck in the door, etc.

The animals went in five by five, by hugging each other they kept alive, etc.

The animals went in six by six, as they went the picked-up sticks, etc.

The animals went in seven by seven, the pig thought he was in heaven, etc.

The animals went in eight by eight, the tortoise thought he might be late, etc.

The animals went in nine by nine, marching along in a straight line.etc.

The animals went in ten by ten; the animals went in ten by ten, hurrah, hurrah,

The animals went in ten by ten; the animals went in ten by ten, hurrah, hurrah,

The last one in was the little red hen.

The animals went in ten by ten, all to get out of the rain.

The sillier you and the children can make the verse, the better the children will like it.

Weight

Children love comparing weights, and you can have a lot of fun weighing pumpkins. Different sized children have a different experience of what heavy means to them.

You can also look at hand size, and this provides an excellent opportunity to talk about age and the stages of growth of the human body.

A suduku puzzle can be printed or created together.

Developing Emerging Literacy
A memory game

Language Development

Collect a selection of Autumn leaves nuts and fruit. Identify each item and talk about the word.

Cover the items with a towel and recall the items under the towel.

Autumn Songs and stories

Songs are a wonderful way to enjoy developing language, and they are also a great way to collaborate and play with your child.

Leaves

The leaves of the trees (Tune: The wheels on the bus)

The leaves on the trees turn orange and red,
Orange and red, orange and red.
The leaves on the trees turn orange and red,
All round the town.

The leaves of the trees come tumbling down,
Tumbling down, tumbling down,
The leaves of the trees come tumbling down,

All round the town.

The leaves of the trees go swish, swish, swish,
Swish, swish, swish, swish, swish, swish,
The leaves of the trees go swish, swish swish,
All round town.

We'll rake them in a pile and jump right in.
Jump right in. jump right in.
We'll rake them in a pile and jump right in,
All round town.

5 little pumpkins

Five little pumpkins sitting on a gate (hold up 5 fingers).

The first one said "Oh my, it is getting late!" (hands on cheeks).

The second one said "There's a chill in the air! (arms around self).

The third one said, "But we don't care!" (swing pointer finger).

The fourth one said, "We are ready for some fun!" (hands in the air).

The fifth one said, "Let's run and run and run!"

So whoooooooooo went the wind, (make a whooo sound).

And out went the lights (clap hands once loudly).

And five little pumpkins rolled out of sight! (roll hands).

Story telling

Story telling is such an important way to develop language and literacy. The book Tree is a beautiful way to immerse yourself and your child in a tree. The book is a peek through picture book, and it discovers the bustling life of a tree. Tree is there in all its glory through the seasons. In Autumn, the animals such as the squirrel and the owl collect food and store it away.

The book is to be enjoyed and read, but you could extend the learning by creating puppets and pretend to be the animals in the tree.

If you do not have a book, you might like to make an owl puppet and just play on a tree.

Owl inspiration

Create a simple Owl puppet with lollipop sticks, glue on leaves and mark the eyes with paint.

Explore sensory letters in leaves.

T for Tree

Pumpkin Soup

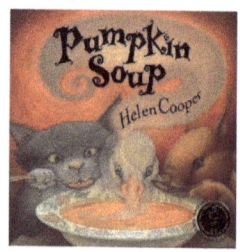

Pumpkin Soup is a favourite book which explores the relationship between three friends, a cat, a duck and a squirrel. They make pumpkin soup together peacefully until they fight, and duck runs away. This is a story of anger, emotions and loss, and it does end happily. The story has beautiful sounds to explore, so making puppets and acting it out would be great fun.

Face Masks

Don't worry if you do not have the book, you can make the puppets and play with a pumpkin in your imaginary cottage in the woods.

Cat Puppet

Materials – What you need

A collection of leaves, paper plates, scissors, lollipop sticks, glue, masking tape and black paint.

Directions

Collect a variety of leaves of different shapes.

Cut the paper plate in the shape of a cat's head.

Glue on the leaves and stick the plate to the lollipop with masking tape.

Paint a colour of your choice.

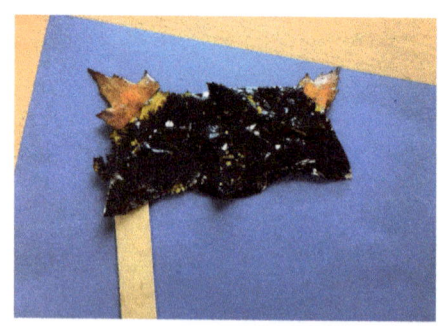

Squirrel Mask

Use a lollipop and arrange leaves in a squirrel shape. Glue on a googly eye.

Wooden Spoon Stories

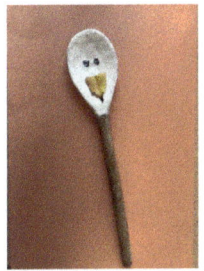

Create a series of wooden spoon puppets. Simply choose an appropriate colour and choose eyes and a beak or nose to create an imaginative puppet for the children to play with.

Explore sensory letters in lentils.

Well Being Activities

Research has shown the great benefits of physical exercise. Physical exercise can boost your self-esteem, mood and sleep quality and it is recommended that young children should be active for at least 3 hours per day. Autumn provides an opportunity for all sorts of active play. Wheelbarrows, swings and piles of leaves can provide hours of fun.

Halloween Fun

Halloween is an important part of Autumn. Mark making on a chalk board.

Sensory Play

Collect leaves, buy some lentils, cut the pumpkin, and let the children feel the different textures. They will have hours of fun pouring and playing with spoons at the Halloween tuff tray.

Sensory Halloween Tuff Tray

A tuff tray is a builder's tray that in recent times has been used in many homes and educational settings for messy play. It is octagonal in shape and perfect for messy play. A tuff tray is easy to carry and store and it can be used on a stand or table or on the ground.

It is time to play with the crowns you made.

Cat Mask

Dragons
Let's make dragons....find dragon parts in nature.

Scales

Eyes

Tails

Claws

FOR THE BOUNTY OF THE EARTH

Autumn is the season when we harvest the beautiful fruits and vegetables in our gardens and it is a season to cherish the bounty and beauty of the earth.

And of course it is always time to play.
Play bob the apple – fill a bucket of water and try to bite the apple.
Paint a pumpkin.

Halloween Bags

Collect all those treats.

Let's have a Halloween teddy bear's picnic.

Simple magic in nature

The Halloween feast does not have to be lots of plastic and new things and junk food, it can be wholesome things done in a new way. Take your feast outside, put the soup in a pumpkin shell. Have a Halloween party at night.

Halloween Feast

Pumpkin Soup

Ingredients
1 pumpkin about 4kg in size.
125g butter.

2 medium onions peeled and finely chopped.

1 cinnamon stick.

Freshly grated nutmeg.

Salt and pepper.

3 pints chicken stock.

Method

1. Scoop the seeds out of the pumpkin and remove the flesh and roughly chop it.
2. Melt the butter in a large pan and add the onions. Cook for 10-15 minutes until they are softened and browned.
3. Add the pumpkin flesh, cinnamon and nutmeg and season with salt and pepper.
4. Increase the heat and cover the pan with a lid. Cook for 40-45 minutes occasionally stirring until the pumpkin is cooked through.
5. Add the stock and bring to the boil.

6. Remove from the heat and cool slightly.

7. Blend the soup in a blender.

8. Pour the soup back into the saucepan and cook on a low simmer for another half an hour.

9. Pour into a pumpkin shell and plan a party outside.

Enjoy a Halloween Feast

Blackcurrant juice, bat apples and of course there are cakes!

The party is even more fun at night time, with lots of leaf lights.

Glue on some leaves to a glass jar and use battery-operated night lights to decorate.

Emotional Activities
Mindfulness activities

Find a beautiful leaf and sit and do a leaf meditation.

Trace your fingers around the leaf – Breathe in, count to 4….. Hold count to 4….. – Breathe Out ……

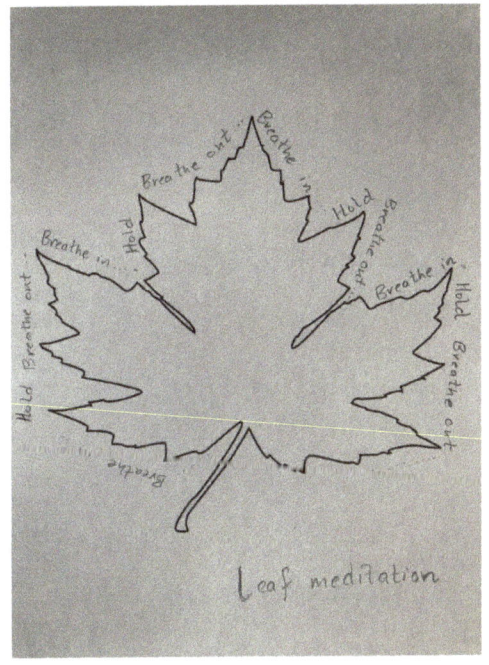

A Thanksgiving Meditation

From your sit spot, reach out your hand, feel the ground, the moss, the leaves, the bark of a tree.

Feel your own hands.

Gently massage your own hands.

In this moment of gentleness, be grateful for you.

Happy Autumn – the season of thanksgiving.

References

Akeson McGurk., L (2017) There is no such thing as bad weather. Touchstone Books, New York. U.S.A.

Barnardos, Willoughby, M., 2014, Outdoor Play Matters resources@barnardos.ie

Bruce Tina, (2007, 4th edition) Developing Learning in Early Education. Sage Publications, U.K.

Bilton H., (1998) Outdoor Play in the Early Years Management and Innovation, London: David Fulton.

Louv R., (2013) Last Child in the Woods, Atlantic Books, U.S.A

Louv. R (2019) Our Wild Calling. Algonquin Books, U.S.A

Roslund, M., Puhakka, R., Gronoos, M. Biodiversity intervention enhances immune regulation and health associated commensal microbiota among day care children. Science Advances 14/10/ 2020 Vol.6 no.42.

Dear Reader,

If you enjoyed this book, would you kindly post a short review on Amazon or Goodreads? Your feedback will make all the difference to getting the word out about this book.

To leave a review, go to Amazon and type in the book title. Please scroll to the bottom of the page to where it says 'Write a Review' and then submit your review.

Thank you in advance.

If you enjoyed this book, you might also like other books in the Thrive series: Spring - Summer - Winter collection for the Early years (2 to 8 years).

www.ingramcontent.com/pod-product-compliance
Lightning Source LLC
Chambersburg PA
CBHW040417100526
44588CB00022B/2857